SMART STRATEGIES FOR
PAYING FOR
COLLEGE

SMART STRATEGIES FOR
PAYING FOR
COLLEGE

G. S. PRENTZAS

ROSEN
PUBLISHING®

New York

Published in 2015 by The Rosen Publishing Group, Inc.
29 East 21st Street, New York, NY 10010

Library of Congress Cataloging-in-Publication Data

Prentzas, G. S.
Smart strategies for paying for college/G. S. Prentzas.—
First edition.
    pages cm.—(Financial security and life success for teens)
Includes bibliographical references and index.
Audience: Grades 7-12.
ISBN 978-1-4777-7614-8 (library bound)—
ISBN 978-1-4777-7616-2 (pbk.)—
ISBN 978-1-4777-7617-9 (6-pack)
1. College costs—United States—Planning—Juvenile
literature. 2. Student aid—United States—Juvenile literature.
3. Education, Higher—United States—Finance—Juvenile
literature. I. Title.
LB2342.P68 2014
378.3—dc23

                                                    2014003040

Manufactured in the United States of America

CONTENTS

INTRODUCTION

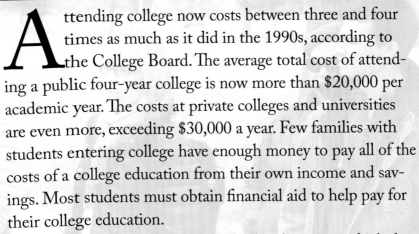

Attending college now costs between three and four times as much as it did in the 1990s, according to the College Board. The average total cost of attending a public four-year college is now more than $20,000 per academic year. The costs at private colleges and universities are even more, exceeding $30,000 a year. Few families with students entering college have enough money to pay all of the costs of a college education from their own income and savings. Most students must obtain financial aid to help pay for their college education.

Financial aid is any grant, scholarship, loan, or paid job that a student receives to help pay college expenses. Many different sources, from federal and state agencies to private enterprises and colleges themselves, provide financial aid to students.

For the average student, grants and scholarships pay for 30 percent of college costs. Parent contributions cover 27 percent, and parent borrowing pays for 9 percent of costs. Student borrowing accounts for 18 percent, and student income and savings pay for 11 percent. Funds from relatives and friends make up the remaining 5 percent.

According to a study sponsored by Sallie Mae, an educational loan company, parental contributions to paying college costs declined from an average of 37 percent in 2010 to 27 percent in 2013. Although the use of funds from college savings plans has increased, students are borrowing more money than ever to make up for lower parent contributions. College

A student *(left)* at Saint Michael's College in Vermont talks with high school students and their parents during a campus tour for prospective students. Because of the high cost of a college education, high school students should start planning how to pay for college education before their senior year.

students now owe, on average, about $25,000 in student loans by the time they graduate. In 2013, total student loan debt in the United States topped $1 trillion. Yes, $1,000,000,000,000!

Although the price of a college education is high, many people believe that the value of a college education surpasses its cost. Employers increasingly require that job applicants have a college degree. A college degree will increase your chance of getting a job after graduation, and, on average, college graduates earn more money than high school graduates. Attending college enables you to meet new people, explore your interests, and learn to live on your own. A college education trains you to think critically and solve problems, and it prepares you for a wide range of careers.

Paying for college is a major task, and applying for financial aid is complicated and time consuming. You must figure out how much it will cost for you to attend the colleges that you want to attend. Then you must estimate how much you and your family can contribute to pay tuition and other college expenses. Financial aid is available from many sources, so you will need to conduct substantial research to find aid programs that you may be eligible for. You will have scholarship, grant, and loan applications to fill out and strict deadlines to meet. You will have financial aid offers from colleges to compare.

The best way to tackle the task of paying for college is to make a detailed plan that breaks down the tasks into achievable steps. Understanding how financial aid works and using smart strategies will help you maximize the amount of financial aid you receive. It will also help lower the amount of debt you will have when you graduate.

CHAPTER 1

FIRST STEPS

Most students and families need help to pay for college. That's where financial aid comes in. The goal for a student seeking assistance to pay for college is to assemble a financial aid package that provides enough money to pay the costs that the student cannot cover.

Financial aid comes in three major types: scholarships and grants, loans, and work-study. Scholarships and grants are educational funds that are free. Students do not have to pay back the money they receive. In most cases, scholarships are awarded on the basis of merit, and grants are awarded on the basis of financial need. Loans are educational funds that a student must pay back, with interest. The federal government sponsors several student loan programs, and banks and other financial institutions offer educational loans. Finally, work-study jobs allow students to earn money to pay college costs while still in school.

HOW FINANCIAL AID WORKS

Financial aid bridges the gap between what a student and his or her family can afford to pay for college and the actual cost of attending the student's college. The difference between college costs and a family's contribution is known as financial need. Financial need is one of the most important concepts in the financial aid universe.

Financial need is estimated by determining two factors. You must first assess the cost of attendance, which is the total amount it will cost you to attend college each year. College costs include

A college student studies in her dorm room. In addition to tuition, fees, books, and other expenses, housing costs are an important factor in determining the total cost of attending college.

tuition, room and board, books and other educational materials, transportation, and other personal and miscellaneous costs for the academic year. Most college financial aid offices provide estimates for these costs. Compare the costs of the colleges that you are considering attending.

Second, you must know your family's expected contribution. Most families contribute some money to pay for college costs. How much depends on a variety of factors. The U.S. Department of Education uses a standard formula to calculate expected family contribution for students seeking financial aid. The calculation of expected family contribution is based primarily on family income, assets, savings, number of children, and number of students attending college.

Many sources that provide financial aid funds use a student's financial need to determine whether the student qualifies for financial aid and how much money an eligible student should receive. Your financial need will vary among prospective colleges because tuition and other costs differ between institutions.

WORKING WITH EXPERTS

Figuring out financial aid is often overwhelming for students and their families. Filling out the necessary financial forms and applying for scholarships, grants, and loans can seem like a full-time job. To make this task easier, it helps to work with experts.

Your family may need to consult with a financial planner or accountant to better understand family finances and the information required by financial aid forms. Financial aid counselors are professionals who specialize in helping families with the financial aid process. Hiring one makes sense for some students and families. Students can also take advantage of the expertise of college financial aid offices. A financial aid officer can answer questions about the financial aid available at the school and help you with aid forms and deadlines that the school may require you to meet. You can also find plenty of good information about the financial aid process online and in books.

Because paying for college is a complex task, some students and parents hire financial experts to help them navigate the financial aid system.

FORMS AND DEADLINES

The first major step in the financial aid process is to complete the Free Application for Federal Student Aid (FAFSA). You can complete this form online or submit a paper form. The FAFSA requires you to provide financial information, such as your family's income and assets. This information allows the U.S. Department of Education to calculate your expected family contribution. Students applying for federal financial aid must

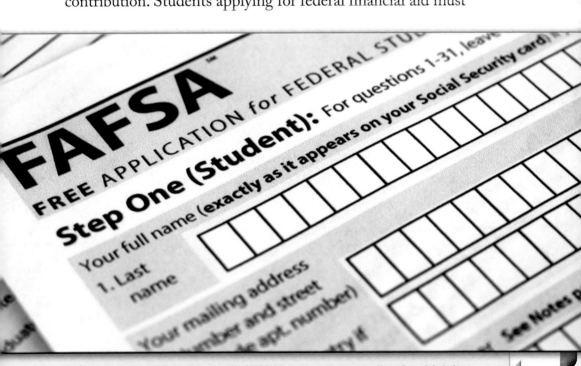

The Free Application for Federal Student Aid (FAFSA) is the most important college financial aid form. Students must fill out the FAFSA to apply for federal financial aid, and many colleges and organizations use information provided on the form to determine eligibility for grants and scholarships.

complete a FAFSA. Many other financial aid sources, such as scholarship programs and college financial aid offices, also use the FAFSA to determine financial aid eligibility and amounts.

You and your family should fill out the FAFSA form as soon as possible after January 1. That's the date when the government releases the form for the next school year. Filing the form online at https://fafsa.ed.gov is easier for most students and families. The website will guide you through the process. The FAFSA requires you to sign up for a personal identification number (PIN), list schools you are considering attending, and provide specific family financial information. Be sure to answer all questions and fill out the form completely.

The Department of Education uses your FAFSA information to produce a Student Aid Report (SAR). It provides a summary of your FAFSA results, including your expected family contribution. The federal government and other financial aid sources use your expected family contribution to determine whether you are eligible for the types of financial aid that are based on a student's financial need, including grants, loans, and work-study programs.

You will receive a copy of your SAR. The colleges you list on your FAFSA form will also receive your SAR. If you fill out the form online, the Department of Education will send your FAFSA information to as many as ten different colleges that you are considering attending. If you fill out a paper form, it will send your information to only four schools.

Your SAR enables colleges to determine whether you qualify for financial aid and, if you do, to prepare a financial aid offer tailored to your circumstances. Because the information in your

THE FAFSA4CASTER

THE FAFSA4CASTER IS A FREE ONLINE TOOL PROVIDED BY THE U.S. DEPARTMENT OF EDUCATION. IT CAN BE ACCESSED THROUGH THE FAFSA WEBSITE. THE FAFSA4CASTER ASKS FOR BASIC INFORMATION, INCLUDING FAMILY INCOME AND SAVINGS. ONCE YOU PROVIDE ALL OF THE REQUESTED DATA, THE FAFSA4CASTER ESTIMATES YOUR ELIGIBILITY FOR FEDERAL STUDENT AID, INCLUDING FEDERAL GRANTS AND LOANS. IT ALSO ESTIMATES YOUR EXPECTED FAMILY CONTRIBUTION.

THE FAFSA4CASTER GIVES YOU AN EARLY ESTIMATE OF YOUR FINANCIAL AID ELIGIBILITY SO THAT YOU AND YOUR FAMILY CAN START PLANNING YOUR FINANCIAL AID STRATEGY. USING THE TOOL DOES NOT QUALIFY YOU FOR ANY FINANCIAL AID. YOU MUST COMPLETE THE FAFSA TO START THE FINANCIAL AID PROCESS.

SAR is confidential, a financial aid office will not share it with any other department at the institution. Confirm that all of the data on your SAR is correct. A college's financial aid office may require you to verify all of the information on your SAR.

For some students, the second major step in the financial aid process is to fill out a CSS/Financial Aid Profile application. As part of their financial aid process, more than three hundred colleges require students to fill out a CSS/Profile to apply for college-based scholarships and grants. Administered by the College Scholarship Service, part of the College Board, the CSS/Profile asks for much more information about family assets and income than the FAFSA.

You can fill out the CSS/Profile application online. You must pay a $24 application fee, which includes the cost of having your CSS/Profile report sent to one college. CSS charges $18 for each additional report.

For most students, particularly those attending private colleges, filling out the CSS/Profile is worth the effort. The schools that require a CSS/Profile usually award students substantial scholarship and grant aid. For example, the average scholarship and grant package at Middlebury College is more than $36,000 a year.

EVALUATING FINANCIAL AID PACKAGES

The colleges that receive your SAR will send you a financial aid offer. A college with higher attendance costs may offer a better financial aid package than a lower-priced college. When acceptance letters start arriving, many students compare financial aid offers when deciding which admissions offer to accept.

College A is offering you more free money in the form of scholarships and grants. It's also offering you work-study aid. Although University B has a lower cost of attendance, it has a higher net cost because it's offering you less scholarship and grant money. To attend University B, you would have to borrow $8,000 the first year to meet the total cost of attendance. If you attend College A, you will have to borrow only $2,500 that year, which will result in lower loan debt when you graduate. Although cost has become an important factor for many

A college's financial aid offer can sometimes be surprising. Because cost is an important factor in attending college, students should compare financial aid offers made by different colleges before making a final decision about which college to attend.

COMPARE THESE TWO SAMPLE FINANCIAL AID OFFERS:

	College A	University B
Cost of attendance	$35,000	$25,000
Grants and scholarships	$25,000	$12,000
Net cost	$10,000	$13,000
Funds to pay net cost:		
Family contribution	$5,000	$5,000
Loans	$2,500	$8,000
Work-study	$2,500	$0

students in deciding which college to attend, you may still prefer to attend University B for other reasons.

CHAPTER 2

FREE MONEY FOR COLLEGE: SCHOLARSHIPS

You've probably heard a lot about college scholarships. There's a good reason. Scholarships are free money. Along with grants, they're the best kind of financial aid because students do not have to repay funds they receive from scholarships. The more scholarship funds you receive, the less money you'll have to borrow or find from other sources.

Scholarships make up a lower percentage of financial aid than most people expect—only about 4 percent. Although that sounds like a small amount, about $3 billion in scholarship funds are awarded each year. There are hundreds of scholarship programs. Scholarships are awarded on the basis of a range of factors, from the ones you would expect—high grades, nearly perfect SAT scores, athletic ability—to the wacky: knowing how to knit, winning a duck-calling contest, or making the best prom outfit out of tape. Most scholarships are competitive, and some are highly competitive. To obtain a scholarship, you must meet the sponsoring organization's

A talented high school athlete may be able to earn a college athletic scholarship to pay all or part of the cost of attending college.

stated requirements and then convince the organization that you're the best candidate among all the applicants.

SCHOLARSHIP BASICS

Most scholarships are merit based. Merit scholarships are awarded to students who meet a scholarship program's specific qualifications. Scholarship qualifications vary greatly. They may be based on criteria ranging from academic or artistic achievement to state residency or parent employment. Some scholarships are based on financial need. Most need-based financial aid comes from federal and state grant programs, but some scholarships are based wholly or in part on financial need.

Many scholarships are aimed at certain groups of people. For example, there are scholarships that are available only to high school seniors or to descendants of the person who funded the scholarship. Some companies offer scholarships to their employees or to children of their employees.

A scholarship is often a one-time award. For example, the Flag Manufacturers Association of America annually awards a total of $2,000 in scholarship money to high school seniors. The scholarship is not renewable. Applicants submit an essay explaining what the U.S. flag means to them. Some scholarships may cover your entire tuition or cost of attendance. For example, each year the Gates Millennium Scholars Program provides one thousand recipients full four-year scholarships to attend any school. Some scholarships include personal and professional development programs. For example, the Morehead-Cain Scholarship at the University of North Carolina offers its recipients a full, four-year scholarship, plus a fully funded summer enrichment program that provides recipients experience in outdoor leadership, public service, inquiry and exploration, and private enterprise.

Scholarships that can be renewed usually have rules or requirements students have to meet to continue receiving the aid. For example, a student may have to maintain a certain grade point average or continue to reside in a specific state

Two high school students *(middle left and middle right)* accept a $5,000 scholarship from the representatives of a large media company. Many corporations sponsor college scholarship programs to reward high-achieving students, and some companies award scholarships to the children of their employees.

to keep receiving funds from a scholarship program. Federal financial aid rules require colleges to take into consideration any scholarship awards when calculating a student's financial aid package. As a result, the $500 you win in a high school scholarship essay contest may be considered as part of your expected family contribution for your freshman year.

FINDING SCHOLARSHIPS

Many different organizations fund scholarship programs. Most colleges provide scholarships to help their students afford tuition and other college costs. College-based scholarships may be awarded on the basis of a variety of factors, including merit, academic major, race, or financial need. Contact the financial aid offices of colleges you're interested in attending. Ask them what scholarships the school offers and request applications for any scholarship for which you may be eligible. Be sure to confirm the application deadlines for all scholarship programs.

College-based scholarships are often the most desirable type of scholarship because they may be awarded annually for four years. These types of scholarships usually have strict requirements for keeping a scholarship from one year to the next. If a scholarship is renewable, ask the financial aid offices about the rules for renewal.

Private organizations are a major source of scholarships. Many corporations, nonprofit foundations, community organizations, and clubs sponsor scholarships. For example, the Posse Foundation awards scholarships to students with extraordinary academic and leadership potential. In most cases, the eligibility requirements for private scholarships are related to the sponsor's business or mission. For example, a company's scholarship program may be open only to the children of employees, or a scholarship from a civic organization may involve writing an essay on a topic related to community service. Many private scholarships are offered for only one year. If you win a one-year scholarship, make plans to replace the scholarship amount with funds from another source the following school year.

Governments are also a source of scholarships. Although the federal government is better known for its large grant programs, it also funds scholarship programs. Federal scholarships

Many local civic organizations offer college scholarships to area students. Being a member of the organization or working as a volunteer for the organization may make a student eligible for a scholarship.

are usually administered by federal agencies. For example, the National Oceanic and Atmospheric Administration supports a scholarship program that awards funds to students training in fields related to oceanic and atmospheric science. The program also funds a summer internship program for scholarship recipients. Some state governments also have scholarship programs. For example, the state of Florida funds the Florida Medallion Scholars program.

ROTC SCHOLARSHIPS

THE RESERVE OFFICERS' TRAINING CORPS (ROTC) SCHOLARSHIP PROGRAM PREPARES STUDENTS FOR CAREERS AS MILITARY OFFICERS. IT PROVIDES STUDENTS WITH A FULL COLLEGE SCHOLARSHIP IN EXCHANGE FOR A COMMITMENT TO SERVE IN THE MILITARY AFTER GRADUATION. THE U.S. ARMY, U.S. AIR FORCE, U.S. NAVY, AND U.S. MARINES OFFER ROTC SCHOLARSHIPS AT HUNDREDS OF COLLEGES.

Two ROTC cadets conduct a tour for prospective students at St. Mary's University in Texas. In exchange for a commitment to serve in the U.S. armed forces, an ROTC scholarship will pay college costs for students accepted into an ROTC program.

STUDENTS ENTERING AN ROTC PROGRAM TAKE ELECTIVE ROTC COURSES DURING THEIR FRESHMAN AND SOPHOMORE YEARS, ALONG WITH STANDARD COLLEGE COURSES. PARTICIPATION IN THE FIRST TWO YEARS OF THE PROGRAM INVOLVES NO OBLIGATION TO SERVE IN THE MILITARY. STUDENTS WHO CHOOSE TO CONTINUE IN THE PROGRAM TAKE ADVANCED ROTC COURSES WHILE COMPLETING THEIR DEGREES. WHEN AN ROTC STUDENT GRADUATES, HE OR SHE IS COMMISSIONED AS AN OFFICER. DEPENDING ON THE CIRCUMSTANCES, THE GRADUATE MAY ENTER ACTIVE MILITARY DUTY OR MAY SERVE WITH THE RESERVES OR NATIONAL GUARD. YOU CAN APPLY FOR AN ROTC SCHOLARSHIP ONLINE AT THE WEBSITES OF THE U.S. ARMY, AIR FORCE, NAVY, AND MARINES.

There are so many scholarships available that it's hard to know where to start searching for the ones that you may be eligible for. To narrow your search, make a personal inventory of characteristics that may qualify you for a scholarship. Do you have top grades and admissions test scores? Are you a member of a minority group? Do you have a special talent or accomplishments in a specific area? Do you have an academic field of study or a career in mind? Do your parents' employers offer scholarships? Are your parents military veterans? Which local nonprofit or civic organizations offer scholarships? Does your state offer scholarships?

Once you've made a list of your characteristics, focus your scholarship search on scholarship programs that may be a good fit for you. Many free sources of information about scholarships are available. Check with your high school guidance counselor and the financial aid offices at colleges you would like to attend. Use the Department of Labor's free scholarship search tool, which can be accessed through the CareerOneStop website. Ask your state's department of education about scholarships. Use your public library's reference section. Contact foundations, civic and community groups, religious organizations, and local businesses to find out whether they offer scholarships. Research ethnicity-based organizations and groups, such as professional associations, that are related to your planned academic field or career interests. Ask your parents whether their employers offer scholarships.

APPLYING FOR SCHOLARSHIPS

Each scholarship program has its own application requirements, so you need to determine the application process for each one. Request an application or download one from the sponsor's website. Read all scholarship applications carefully and fill them out completely. Start a financial aid calendar and input deadline dates for all scholarships and other types of financial aid. Keep in mind that some scholarships require that you apply before you start your senior year of high school.

Information or materials in addition to an application are required by many scholarship programs. These include your high school transcript, standardized test scores, Student Aid

Report, and letters of recommendation. You may also have to write an essay that describes why you should be awarded the scholarship or interview with a scholarship committee. If you are applying for a talent-based award, such as a musical or other performance scholarship, you may have to audition for the scholarship sponsor.

If you are awarded a scholarship, you will likely receive a check directly from the sponsor. In some cases, the sponsor may send scholarship funds to your college, where they will be deposited in your account. You can then use the funds from the account to pay tuition and other expenses.

CHAPTER 3

EVEN MORE FREE MONEY: GRANTS

L ike scholarships, grants are awards of free money that students use to pay college expenses. A student receiving a grant does not have to pay back the money. The purpose of grants is to ensure students can get a college education by providing funds to help them meet their total college costs.

GRANTS BASICS

Unlike scholarships, grants are not awarded primarily on academic merit or outstanding skill. They are awarded primarily on the basis of financial need. To receive a grant, you will have to demonstrate that you have financial need to pay your school's cost of attendance. Grants come from a variety of sources, including governments, schools, and private organizations.

FEDERAL GRANTS

The federal government funds several educational grant programs. The federal Pell Grant is available for undergraduate

Grants are a type of financial aid based mostly on a student's financial need. Grants help students who may not otherwise be able to afford to attend college.

students who demonstrate financial need. The amount you receive depends on your financial need, your cost of attendance, and whether you attend school full-time or part-time. The amount of any other financial aid you receive does not affect the amount of your Pell Grant.

To receive a Pell Grant, you must complete the FAFSA. The U.S. Department of Education administers the Pell

29

Grant program, so there is no other form to fill out to apply. The Department of Education will inform you if you qualify for a Pell Grant. Students with low expected family contribution amounts usually qualify for Pell Grants.

If you qualify for a Pell Grant, the federal government sends the amount of the grant to your school. The school places the funds in your account, and you can pay your educational expenses with the money. Not all schools participate in the Pell Grant program, so check with your school's financial aid office to confirm that it does.

The Federal Supplemental Educational Opportunity Grant (FSEOG) provides financial aid to students who have extreme financial need. It is available to undergraduates only. To apply for this grant, you must fill out the FAFSA so your college can determine your financial need. Individual colleges administer the FSEOG program on their campuses. Not all schools participate, so check with your school's financial aid office to confirm that your school offers FSEOGs.

The federal Teacher Education Assistance for College and Higher Education (TEACH) Grant provides funding for students who agree to accept certain types of teaching positions following graduation. Participants must sign a contract agreeing to serve in a qualified teaching position for four years. To qualify for a TEACH Grant, a student must take the coursework necessary to become an elementary or secondary school teacher. Students receiving TEACH Grants must maintain a certain grade point average. If a student does not fulfill the contract, TEACH funds given to the student will be converted to a federal student loan. The student would then have to repay the amount.

College students interested in pursuing a teaching career may qualify for the TEACH Grant. This federal program provides grants to students who agree to take education courses and teach in certain schools after they graduate.

The teaching position taken by a TEACH Grant recipient must be in a school with a critical shortage of teachers or be in a high-need field. The U.S. Department of Education designates the schools and fields that qualify for students to fulfill their TEACH Grant obligations. For example, teaching at a school operated by the federal Bureau of Indian Affairs satisfies this TEACH requirement. Current high-need fields for TEACH Grants include math, science, special education, and bilingual education.

Students whose parent or guardian died as a result of military service in Iraq or Afghanistan may qualify for the Iraq and Afghanistan Service Grant. For this grant, a student must be ineligible for a Pell Grant because of having less financial need than the Pell Grant program requires. The student also must have been younger than twenty-four at the time of the parent's death.

STATE GRANTS

Many states also offer educational grants that students do not have to repay. State-funded grants usually provide funds for low-income students. Some grants are aimed at providing funds for students who are training for specific jobs, such as teaching or nursing. State-funded grants aim to boost the state's economy and encourage college students pursuing high-need careers to remain in the state.

State grant programs differ from state to state. Research the grant programs offered by your state. Most state grants require that the recipient be a long-term resident of the state. Many students find that using state grants and scholarships to pay the lower tuition for state residents at a public university in their own state substantially reduces the total cost of attending college.

To apply for the Minnesota State Grant Program, for example, a student must complete the FAFSA. The student must be a Minnesota resident and a secondary school graduate, or equivalent. A Minnesota State Grant cannot be used at an out-of-state school. It must be used at an eligible institution in Minnesota. The state's public universities, community colleges, and public technical colleges—along with most private colleges and some private career institutions—are eligible.

State administrators determine the amount of a Minnesota State Grant by taking into account a student's cost of attendance, expected family contribution, federal grants, and other financial aid amounts. A student may reapply for a Minnesota State Grant each academic year. An initial two-semester grant may be renewed for up to six full-time semesters. The student must also make satisfactory progress and demonstrate financial need to requalify for the grant.

COLLEGE GRANTS

In addition to qualifying for federal and state grants, students may qualify for a grant from the college they are attending. College grants are usually based on financial need, but they do not have the strict income criteria that most government grants have.

Colleges award their grants to certain students as a supplement to government educational grants. These grants make these colleges more affordable for students. Colleges may award grants to attract certain students to their campuses. For example, a college's grant program may be aimed at attracting more women, racial minorities, or other defined groups of students. College grants often supplement athletic scholarships that do not pay a student–athlete's total cost of attendance. Many private colleges use grants to attract talented students they want to recruit.

A Penn State defender trips up a University of Nebraska ball carrier. Grants help students with partial athletic scholarships bridge the gap between their family contribution and their cost of attending college.

Some college-based grant programs are open to all students. These are known as general grants and are usually awarded based on financial need and academic performance. Other grants are aimed at diversifying the student body. Student-specific grants are usually designed for low-income or disadvantaged students or students from military families. Colleges fund subject-specific grants to attract students pursuing degrees in specific fields, such as science, health care, engineering, or the arts.

PRIVATE ORGANIZATION GRANTS

SOME COLLEGE GRANT FUNDS ARE AVAILABLE FROM THE PRIVATE SECTOR. CORPORATIONS AND PROFESSIONAL ASSOCIATIONS OFFER GRANTS FOR DESERVING STUDENTS WHO ARE PURSUING DEGREES THAT ARE CLOSELY RELATED TO THE BUSINESS OR ORGANIZATION. RELIGIOUS ORGANIZATIONS, AS WELL AS COMMUNITY SERVICE GROUPS, ALSO SPONSOR COLLEGE GRANT PROGRAMS. THESE ORGANIZATIONS USUALLY HAVE SPECIFIC ELIGIBILITY REQUIREMENTS.

A group of teens meets at their church. Some religious organizations offer educational grants to college students. If you or your parents are members of or volunteer for a community organization, find out whether it sponsors a college grant program.

APPLYING FOR GRANTS

Although searching for grants is a time-consuming process, the reward of free money for college is enticing. Assess the qualities you have that may qualify you for a grant. Are you an undergraduate or graduate student? What is your field of interest? What are your personal attributes, such as race and gender? Are you or your parents members of a union, community group, or other organization? What field of study or career do you anticipate entering?

As with scholarships, the first step to apply for grants is to complete the FAFSA. Federal grants, most state grants, and some college and private grants use the FAFSA to determine your eligibility. If you're applying for a college grant, ask your school's financial aid office about the forms you need and deadline dates. If you're applying for a private grant, ask the grant sponsor about the forms needed and deadlines.

MYTHS AND FACTS

MYTH: APPLYING FOR FINANCIAL AID WILL AFFECT MY CHANCES OF BEING ADMITTED TO COLLEGES.

FACT: FEW COLLEGES CONSIDER AN APPLICANT'S FINANCIAL AID STATUS WHEN MAKING ADMISSION DECISIONS.

MYTH: MY FIRST-CHOICE COLLEGE IS REALLY EXPENSIVE, SO I SHOULDN'T BOTHER APPLYING THERE.

FACT: IT'S USUALLY EASIER TO DEMONSTRATE FINANCIAL NEED WHEN THE COST OF ATTENDANCE IS HIGHER. STUDIES HAVE SHOWN THAT THE AVERAGE INCOME OF FAMILIES OF STUDENTS ATTENDING PRIVATE COLLEGES IS LOWER THAN THE AVERAGE INCOME OF STUDENTS ATTENDING PUBLIC UNIVERSITIES.

MYTH: MY FAMILY'S INCOME IS TOO HIGH TO QUALIFY FOR FINANCIAL AID, SO I DON'T NEED TO APPLY FOR FINANCIAL AID.

FACT: EVEN IF YOUR FAMILY'S INCOME IS TOO HIGH TO QUALIFY FOR A FEDERAL, NEED-BASED GRANT, YOU SHOULD APPLY FOR FINANCIAL AID. YOU MAY QUALIFY FOR A STATE GRANT, A SUBSIDIZED FEDERAL LOAN, OR WORK-STUDY.

CHAPTER 4

CREDIT CARD

CREDIT

OME

ST

BORROWING FROM YOUR UNCLE SAM

The combination of family and personal funds, scholarships, and grants does not cover the costs of college for many students. Education loans are a common way to help pay for college. Even if you don't have a rich uncle who will lend you money, you can borrow from Uncle Sam, the U.S. government. Nearly 40 percent of all financial aid dollars awarded to undergraduates are in the form of federal educational loans.

The federal government sponsors two types of student loan programs. The William D. Ford Direct Loan Program is the largest. It is called a direct program because the U.S. Department of Education lends money directly to students. The Federal Perkins Loan Program is the other type of federal student loan program. It is an indirect program. Colleges, rather than the federal government, offer these loans to students.

DIRECT LOAN PROGRAMS

There are four types of federal direct education loans: direct subsidized loans, direct unsubsidized loans, Direct PLUS

Loans, and direct consolidation loans. Students who demonstrate financial need may apply for direct subsidized loans, which are commonly called direct subsidized Stafford Loans, to help them pay college costs. These loans are considered subsidized because the federal government pays the amount of interest due while the student is enrolled in school. These loans also have a lower interest rate than direct unsubsidized loans. The federal government provides funds to cover the difference. The U.S. Department of Education also provides

To pay for college, many students must take out educational loans. Unlike a scholarship or a grant, the funds from an educational loan must be repaid, usually once a student graduates.

loans to graduate or professional students to pay educational expenses not covered by other financial aid. These are known as Direct PLUS Loans. Parents of a dependent undergraduate student enrolled at least half-time at a participating school may also be eligible for a Direct PLUS Loan.

Undergraduate, graduate, and professional students may also receive direct unsubsidized loans. These loans are called unsubsidized because the borrower must pay the entire amount of interest due on the loan. The federal government pays none of the interest. Students do not need to demonstrate financial need to be eligible for direct unsubsidized loans. Many students receive both direct subsidized loans and direct unsubsidized loans to pay college costs. Finally, direct consolidation loans allow students to combine all federal student loans into a single loan. This program provides a major benefit for borrowers. It allows students to deal with one loan servicer instead of several servicers. They have to make payments to only one company once their student loans are consolidated.

ELIGIBILITY REQUIREMENTS

To be eligible for a federal educational loan, you need to meet certain requirements. You must be a U.S. citizen or a permanent U.S. resident. Noncitizens who meet specific qualifications may also be eligible. In general, if you are a noncitizen student who intends to become a U.S. citizen or permanent resident, you may be eligible for this type of loan. You must comply with federal Selective Service registration requirements.

You must also have a high school diploma or a GED certificate, attend college on at least a half-time basis, and be working toward an eligible degree or certificate. Additionally, you must satisfy the academic progress requirements determined by your college. You can also become ineligible for federal educational loans if you are in default on any student loan or owe a refund on any state or federal grant. If you are in default, you may be able to reestablish your eligibility by meeting the requirements of the Federal Loan Rehabilitation Program.

THE APPLICATION PROCESS

To apply for direct or indirect federal education loans, you must complete the FAFSA. Using your FAFSA information, colleges

A student discusses financial aid options with a college financial aid officer. Your college's financial aid office will answer your questions about financial aid and help you apply for scholarships, grants, and loans.

will first determine your eligibility for a direct subsidized loan. Next, they will determine your eligibility for a direct unsubsidized loan. Some colleges require additional financial aid forms, so check with your prospective colleges' financial aid offices to find out whether you need to fill out more forms. Also ask about the deadlines for submitting these forms.

ESTIMATING YOUR FEDERAL DIRECT LOAN ELIGIBILITY

USE THE NUMBERS GENERATED BY THE **FAFSA** AND THE AMOUNTS OF FINANCIAL AID FROM OTHER SOURCES TO ESTIMATE HOW MUCH MONEY YOU MAY BE ELIGIBLE TO BORROW UNDER FEDERAL STUDENT LOAN PROGRAMS. KEEP IN MIND THAT FOR BOTH SUBSIDIZED AND UNSUBSIDIZED LOAN PROGRAMS, YOUR LOAN AMOUNT MAY NOT EXCEED THE PROGRAM'S MAXIMUM LIMIT. HERE'S THE FORMULA TO ESTIMATE THE AMOUNT OF FEDERAL LOANS YOU MAY BE ELIGIBLE TO RECEIVE:

COST OF ATTENDANCE – EXPECTED FAMILY CONTRIBUTION – OTHER FINANCIAL AID (SCHOLARSHIPS, GRANTS, WORK-STUDY) = AMOUNT OF SUBSIDIZED STAFFORD LOAN ELIGIBILITY.

FOR EXAMPLE, ASSUME THE COST OF ATTENDANCE FOR YOUR FIRST YEAR OF COLLEGE IS $25,000, YOUR EXPECTED FAMILY CONTRIBUTION IS $5,000, AND YOUR OTHER SOURCES OF FINANCIAL AID WILL

AMOUNT TO $14,000. YOUR TOTAL FEDERAL DIRECT LOAN ELIGIBILITY WILL BE $6,000 BECAUSE $25,000 – $5,000 (FAMILY CONTRIBUTION) – $14,000 (GRANTS AND SCHOLARSHIPS) = $6,000. FRESHMEN CAN BORROW A MAXIMUM OF $3,500 UNDER THE SUBSIDIZED STAFFORD LOAN PROGRAM, SO YOU MAY NEED AN UNSUBSIDIZED FEDERAL STAFFORD LOAN TO MEET YOUR COST OF ATTENDANCE. HERE'S THE FORMULA TO ESTIMATE YOUR ELIGIBILITY FOR AN UNSUBSIDIZED FEDERAL STAFFORD LOAN:

COST OF ATTENDANCE – EXPECTED FAMILY CONTRIBUTION – OTHER FINANCIAL AID – SUBSIDIZED FEDERAL STAFFORD LOAN = AMOUNT OF UNSUBSIDIZED STAFFORD LOAN ELIGIBILITY.

USING THE SAME NUMBERS AND ASSUMING YOU ARE ELIGIBLE FOR A SUBSIDIZED STAFFORD LOAN, YOUR UNSUBSIDIZED STAFFORD LOAN ELIGIBILITY WILL BE $2,500, BECAUSE $25,000 – $5,000 – $14,000 – $3,500 = $2,500.

THE LOAN PROCESS

When a college's financial aid office determines that you are eligible for a federal direct loan, it will submit your student loan information to the U.S. Department of Education. The exact amount of the loan depends on several factors, primarily the total cost of attendance and your family's expected contribution. Like other types of loans, student loans have two elements: principal and interest. The principal is the amount of the loan. Interest is a finance charge, or fee, that a lender charges for borrowing money. Interest is usually expressed as a rate, or percentage. The interest rates on federal educational loans are variable, but by law they cannot exceed 8.25 percent. Each year on July 1, the Department of Education adjusts the interest rate for educational loans.

The term, or length, of the loan depends on how much you borrow and which repayment plan you choose. The loan term for federal direct student loans may not exceed thirty years. A student borrower must repay the loan in installments by the end of the loan's term.

Once your loan has been approved by the U.S. Department of Education, you must complete and sign a promissory note. With this legal document, you agree to repay the total loan amount, which equals the principal plus the finance charge.

The Department of Education will disburse, or send, your loan funds to your college on your behalf. The federal government charges a fee of 1.05 percent for disbursing educational loans. For example, if you receive a $3,000 direct subsidized loan, the disbursement fee will be $31.50. This fee is deducted from the amount of your loan. So in this example, your school will receive a loan disbursement of $2,968.50. This fee helps the loan program recover its losses when some students fail to repay their educational loans.

The Department of Education usually sends direct federal loan funds to colleges in two installments. The college then transfers the money to your student account, usually at the beginning of each semester or other school term. Check with your college's financial aid office to learn about its specific transfer policies.

REPAYING YOUR LOAN

Students must start repaying the principal of their subsidized or unsubsidized federal loans six months after they graduate. However, you will be responsible for the interest on your loans during this six-month grace period. For subsidized federal loans, you do not have to make interest payments during the grace period. The amount of interest accrued during the grace period is added to the principal of your loan. Unsubsidized federal loans do not give borrowers a grace period for making interest payments. You must start making interest payments as soon as you graduate. If you drop below half-time enrollment, you must start repaying federal educational loans immediately.

The Department of Education assigns student loans to a loan servicer, a company that handles the billing and other services related to your student loan. The designated loan servicer will contact you after your school makes its first transfer of funds into your student account. The loan servicer will send you periodic statements showing the amounts disbursed under your loan. Once you graduate, you will make your loan payments to the loan servicer. Most student loans have a standard repayment plan. You make a set monthly payment throughout the term of the loan.

Once your federal student loan becomes active, visit the National Student Loan Data System website to find contact information for the loan servicer for your federal loans. You can also view all of the information about your loan, including disbursements to your school. You will need your Federal Student Aid PIN to access this information.

The National Student Loan Data System allows students to view their loan information online. It also allows a borrower to confirm payments once loan repayment has begun.

INDIRECT LOAN PROGRAM

The Federal Perkins Loan Program helps college students who have exceptional financial need pay the costs of their education. It is an indirect loan program because individual colleges and career schools, rather than the U.S. Department of Education, serve as the lenders. These institutions receive

STATE LOAN PROGRAMS

UNCLE SAM IS NOT THE ONLY SOURCE OF GOVERNMENT EDUCATIONAL LOANS. SOME STATES OFFER STUDENT LOANS TO THEIR RESIDENTS. FOR EXAMPLE, THE TEXAS HIGHER EDUCATION COORDINATING BOARD PROVIDES LOANS TO STUDENTS WHO ARE RESIDENTS OF TEXAS AND WHO ARE ELIGIBLE TO PAY IN-STATE TUITION. IT ADMINISTERS TWO LOAN PROGRAMS: THE COLLEGE ACCESS LOAN PROGRAM AND THE TEXAS B-ON-TIME LOAN PROGRAM. ELIGIBILITY REQUIREMENTS, APPLICATION AND LOAN PROCESSES, AND REPAYMENT RULES VARY GREATLY AMONG STATE LOAN PROGRAMS. KEEP IN MIND THAT STATE STUDENT LOAN PROGRAMS ARE USUALLY MORE VULNERABLE TO BUDGET CUTS THAN THE FEDERAL LOAN PROGRAMS.

federal money to start a Perkins Loan program. Each school's Perkins Loan fund is replenished primarily by students repaying their Perkins Loans. The U.S. Department of Education also provides schools with money to cover the costs of certain types of loan cancellations.

ELIGIBILITY REQUIREMENTS

Undergraduate, graduate, and professional students may be eligible for Perkins Loans. In addition to satisfying the citizenship and other requirements of the direct federal educational loan programs, a student must attend a college or an occupational school that participates in the Federal Perkins Loan Program. About 1,700 institutions provide Perkins Loans to students.

THE APPLICATION PROCESS

To apply for a Perkins Loan, students must submit an FAFSA. Using the FAFSA information, a college participating in the program will determine whether you qualify for a Perkins loan at that institution.

THE LOAN PROCESS

Once approved for a Perkins Loan, a student must sign a promissory note to receive the loan. Undergraduates are eligible for a maximum of $5,500 each year. The total amount you can borrow is capped at $27,500. Graduate and professional students can receive up to $8,000 per year, and their total loan amount cannot exceed $60,000. Perkins Loans are the least expensive federal educational loans. The interest rate is set at 5 percent.

The college will apply Perkins Loan funds to your tuition, fees, room and board, and other school expenses. If any Perkins Loan funds remain after these payments, your school will give you a refund. You must use these funds to pay for your other educational expenses. Unlike direct federal student loans, Perkins Loans have no fees for disbursement. However, if you miss a payment or make a late payment, you may have to pay a late charge.

REPAYING YOUR PERKINS LOAN

Recipients of Perkins Loans make no loan payments while they are enrolled in school at least half-time. Payments start nine months after you graduate, leave school, or drop below half-time enrollment. Perkins borrowers repay their loans by sending loan payments directly to their colleges or to a college's loan servicer.

College students who become teachers or nurses may qualify for a U.S. Department of Education program that cancels all or part of the Perkins Loans that they received to pay for college.

Perkins Loans are popular with aspiring teachers and students who intend to enter certain other professional fields, such as nursing or law enforcement. All or part of Perkins Loans may be cancelled if the student meets the qualifications for a specific cancellation program. For example, a borrower who teaches in a school with a high concentration of students from low-income families may cancel his or her outstanding loan over a five-year period. The U.S. Department of Education determines which schools meet this requirement.

CHAPTER 5

MEET YOUR BANKER

I f your scholarships, grants, and federally subsidized loans do not meet your cost of attendance, you may need to borrow money from a private lender. Banks and other financial institutions, as well as some private foundations, offer educational loans. Most students should seek a private loan only after they have borrowed the maximum amount from the federal Stafford Loan program. Students should also compare the terms of private loans with those of the federal PLUS loan program. Private loans usually come with higher interest rates than federally subsidized loans, and the repayment rules are often less flexible.

PRIVATE EDUCATIONAL LOANS BASICS

Students use funds from private educational loans to pay for tuition, books, and other costs of attendance. Private loans are credit based, which means that a lender will approve a loan based on the student's credit score. Credit scores come from credit-reporting agencies, or credit bureaus. These companies

Private educational loans are usually less desirable than federally subsidized loans because they have higher interest rates. As a result, a student will have a higher amount to pay off.

collect information from lenders about their credit customers to create credit histories for individuals. Using a person's credit history, credit-reporting agencies use a formula to produce a credit score. A person's credit score shows how he or she has managed debts. For example, if a person borrows money from a bank to pay for her car and makes her car loan payments on time every month, her credit score would likely increase over time. If she failed to make payments, such as for credit card bills, on time, her credit score would likely decrease.

51

Because most young people have little, if any, credit history, most private educational loans are based on the credit history of a student's parents. Parents often must cosign an educational loan, agreeing to pay off the loan if their child fails to repay the bank.

Because most college students are young and have little, if any, credit history, many private educational loans involve a cosigner. The cosigner agrees to be responsible for the loan if the primary borrower, the student, fails to pay back the loan. In most instances, parents cosign educational loans for their children. In some cases, a student's grandparent or other relative will cosign an educational loan. The lending institution considers the cosigner's credit history when deciding whether to approve the loan.

529 PLANS

A 529 PLAN IS A COLLEGE SAVINGS PLAN SPONSORED BY ALL FIFTY STATES AND SOME PRIVATE COLLEGES AND UNIVERSITIES. AUTHORIZED BY SECTION 529 OF THE FEDERAL INTERNAL REVENUE CODE, FUNDS PLACED INTO A 529 PLAN ARE NOT SUBJECT TO FEDERAL OR STATE TAX AS LONG AS THEY ARE USED TO PAY COLLEGE COSTS. CONTRIBUTIONS MADE TO A 529 PLAN WILL HELP YOU LOWER THE AMOUNT OF PRIVATE LOANS NEEDED TO PAY COLLEGE COSTS.

THERE ARE TWO TYPES OF 529 PLANS. COLLEGE SAVINGS PLANS ALLOW A FAMILY TO CREATE A SAVINGS ACCOUNT FOR A STUDENT. THE FAMILY CAN CHOOSE HOW THE MONEY IN THE ACCOUNT IS INVESTED. WHEN THE STUDENT ENTERS COLLEGE, THE FUNDS IN THE ACCOUNT ARE USED TO PAY COLLEGE COSTS. PREPAID TUITION PLANS ALLOW FAMILIES TO PURCHASE CREDITS AT PARTICIPATING COLLEGES FOR A STUDENT'S FUTURE TUITION. STATE GOVERNMENTS SPONSOR MOST OF THESE PLANS AND REQUIRE PARTICIPANTS TO BE RESIDENTS OF THAT STATE.

Unlike federal educational loans, most private loans are not subsidized. This means that the borrower pays the entire cost of the loan. Interest rates and other terms for private loans vary. Banks and other financial institutions usually offer educational loans with the highest interest rates. Some private foundations and organizations offer lower interest rates. Some colleges also have loan programs that offer lower interest rates than private financial institutions.

The interest rate for private loans can be fixed or variable. A fixed interest rate means that the interest rate is set for the entire term of the loan. A fixed rate provides predictable repayment amounts. However, because lenders assume the risk of losing money if interest rates go up in the future, they often charge fees or higher interest rates for fixed-interest loans.

A variable interest rate means that the interest rate charged may go up or down during the term of the loan, depending on market conditions. The rate charged on a variable rate loan is based on either of two interest rate indexes: the Prime Index or the London Interbank Offered Rate Index. The interest rate of the student loan will change periodically if the relevant index's rate changes. The borrower may have a low introductory interest rate, but the interest rate, and the cost of the loan, may rise significantly in the future.

THE PRIVATE LOAN PROCESS

If you think you may need to borrow money to pay for college, ask your college's financial aid officer for advice. Then research the various educational loans that are available. The terms and conditions of private loans differ. Compare the interest rates, fees, repayment rules, and borrower benefits that each loan offers. Use an online student loan comparison calculator to determine the actual total cost of each loan you're considering.

RESEARCHING LOANS

There are several key factors to consider when researching private student loans. Variable interest rates change over time, so a variable rate can be riskier than a fixed rate. Loans with a

Because private loans have different interest rates and other terms, students should determine the total costs of loan offers—which they can do with the help of an online loan calculator—before deciding which loan to accept.

variable interest rate often start with a lower interest rate. Loan fees also add to the total cost of a loan. Some loans require the payment of an origination fee, which is a fee that the bank levies to process the loan. Look for loans with no origination fee. If you are considering a loan with an origination fee, consider the expense when calculating the total cost of the loan.

Repayment terms are an important consideration when thinking about a loan. Some private student loans allow you to defer payments until after graduation. Others, however, require you to make monthly payments while you are still in school. Although choosing a loan with a longer repayment period will result in lower monthly payments, the total cost of this loan will be more than the total cost of a loan with a shorter repayment period. That's because you will be paying interest for a longer period of time. Choose a loan that gives you enough flexibility so that your monthly payments are not likely to be a burden but that also keeps the total cost of your loan at a reasonable level.

When comparing private loans, take into account any benefits that lenders offer. For example, many banks offer a reduced interest rate if the borrower agrees to allow the bank to deduct monthly loan payments directly from the borrower's checking or savings account at that bank. This option also saves you the hassle of making a payment each month or missing a payment. You must make sure you always have enough money in the account to cover the payments, however.

Compare each loan's annual percentage rate (APR). This figure takes into account the interest rates, fees, length of deferment (if any), and repayment period. Although APR is a useful tool, it does not take into account any borrower benefits and loan discounts, so you must compare these factors separately.

APPLYING FOR A LOAN

Once you have determined which lending institution offers the best private loan for your circumstances, ask the lender for a loan application. Fill out the application and authorize the lender to check your credit score. Cosigners must sign a form allowing the lender to check their credit scores.

Using the credit ratings and the information on your application, the lender's loan officer will approve or deny your loan request. If a lender rejects your application, you can apply for a loan from another private lender. If your application is approved, the lender will draft a promissory note, which is a legal document that provides the terms of the loan.

REPAYING YOUR LOAN

By signing the lender's promissory note, you become legally responsible for repaying the loan. Unlike federal student loans, the loan will not be paid off by the federal government if you default. Student loans are also not discharged, or dismissed, if you later file for bankruptcy. Repayment periods for private educational loan terms vary, but a common period to repay the loan's principal and interest is fifteen years, starting six months after you graduate or quit school. Always make your monthly payments on time to avoid late fees.

10 GREAT QUESTIONS
TO ASK YOUR LENDER

1. Is the interest rate fixed or variable?
2. How can I get a lower interest rate?
3. Is there a discount for already being your customer, such as one for having a checking account?
4. Do you offer a discount on the interest rate once I graduate?
5. What fees do I have to pay?
6. What is the length of the loan?
7. How much will this loan cost in total?
8. Will I need a cosigner?
9. When will my payments start?
10. What will my monthly payments be?

CHAPTER 6

WORKING YOUR WAY THROUGH COLLEGE

Scholarships, grants, and loans do not provide enough money for some students to attend college. If you find yourself in this situation, you may be able to earn money to help pay for your education by participating in a work-study program administered by your school. Some students opt for off-campus jobs working for private employers. Working while going to school can be difficult to manage. You have to juggle classes and schoolwork with job commitments, plus you need time to fulfill family responsibilities, hang out with friends, and relax.

WORK-STUDY PROGRAMS

There are two types of work-study programs: federal work-study and nonfederal work-study. Only U.S. citizens who have received a work-study allocation in their financial aid packages are eligible for federal work-study positions. Some schools also offer nonfederal work-study jobs. These positions are open to any student, regardless of financial aid situation or citizenship.

FEDERAL WORK-STUDY PROGRAM

Most students who receive work-study aid participate in the Federal Work-Study Program. In this program, the U.S. government provides funds for part-time jobs for students who have financial need. Federal work-study is available to undergraduate, graduate, and professional students. Both full-time and part-time students can qualify for the Federal Work-Study Program.

More than 3,400 educational institutions participate in the Federal Work-Study Program. Each institution administers the work-study program on its campus. The program allows students to earn money to help pay educational expenses. It also promotes work related to a student's academic field or work that involves community service.

Federal work-study jobs can be either on campus or off campus. If you have an on-campus job, you'll probably work for your college. Most off-campus employers who participate in the Federal Work-Study Program are either government agencies or private nonprofit organizations. Some private, for-profit employers also participate in the Federal Work-Study Program.

Under the Federal Work-Study Program, the hourly wages paid to students must be at least the federal minimum wage. Employers usually pay about half of the student's wages, and the federal government funds the other half. The lower labor cost benefits employers, making federal work-study student employees attractive to them.

The federal government requires colleges to use at least 7 percent of their federal work-study funds to support students working in community service jobs, such as reading or math tutors for elementary school students. For a federal work-study student to work for a private employer, the federal government requires that the job be related to the student's course of study. For example, a computer science major could work as a computer technician for a private employer.

A college student tutors an elementary school student. Some federal work-study jobs, such as tutoring, are related to community service.

Educational institutions participating in the Federal Work-Study Program use the FAFSA, along with additional forms and documents the school's financial aid office may require, to determine a student's eligibility for federal work-study. You must mark "Yes" to the FAFSA question asking whether you are interested in student employment in order to be considered for the Federal Work-Study Program. To keep

Work-study programs try to ensure that work commitments do not overburden students. These programs place a limit on the number of hours a student can work each week so that students have enough time to attend classes, study, and relax.

participating in federal work-study, a student must submit a new FAFSA each academic year.

A student's total federal work-study award depends primarily on the student's level of need and how much federal funding the student's school has. Even if a student is financially eligible for federal work-study, he or she may not receive federal work-study aid if the school does not have enough federal funds to offer a job to all qualified students. Financial aid offices place eligible students who are not hired for a federal work-study position on a waiting list.

A student participating in the Federal Work-Study Program cannot earn more money than his or her total federal work-study award. The student's employer takes into account the student's total annual award and class commitments when determining the student's work schedule. Most federal work-study students work an average of ten to fifteen hours per week. To ensure that students are not overburdened by their work-study jobs, many schools have a limit on the number of hours a student can work in any given week. Working hours are usually flexible, but students should keep in mind that schoolwork is the top priority.

NONFEDERAL WORK-STUDY PROGRAMS

If you do not qualify for the Federal Work-Study Program, you may have another option. Your school may also offer nonfederal work-study jobs. These programs differ from federal work-study in two important aspects. They are not based on need or on citizenship. All students are eligible for nonfederal work-study jobs.

WORK-STUDY STORIES

KYRA BANNISTER, A STUDENT AT THE UNIVERSITY OF OREGON, DISCUSSED HER WORK-STUDY EXPERIENCE WITH A *U.S. NEWS AND WORLD REPORT* MAGAZINE REPORTER. SHE SAID THAT THE COMBINATION OF WORK AND STUDY SOMETIMES MADE HER "A LITTLE MORE SLEEP DEPRIVED." SHE ASSERTED THAT HER "ACADEMICS DID NOT SUFFER FROM IT." SHE MET MANY OTHER STUDENTS WHILE WORKING AT A COFFEE SHOP. "HAVING A JOB IS AMAZING AND I HIGHLY RECOMMEND IT," BANNISTER SAID. HOWEVER, AMBER BANIKE, A STUDENT AT THE UNIVERSITY OF WISCONSIN–PARKSIDE, STRUGGLED TO BALANCE WORK, SCHOOL, AND FAMILY COMMITMENTS. SHE TOLD THE *MILWAUKEE JOURNAL SENTINEL*, "I'M EITHER AT WORK OR SCHOOL, AND I DON'T HAVE TIME TO DO HOMEWORK."

Through their nonfederal work-study programs, educational institutions try to find students to work in fields related to their field of study. Most of these jobs require specific skills and can be highly competitive. Employers pay all of the student's salary, so they hire only the most talented people.

To find a nonfederal work-study job, check with your major department or with your school's career services department for a listing of positions. Nonfederal work-study jobs have an additional financial consideration. Your earnings from a nonfederal work-study job will be considered as income and used to determine your financial need when your FAFSA is processed the following year.

PRIVATE EMPLOYMENT

Many students do not qualify for federal work-study or their schools do not offer enough work-study jobs. To help pay college expenses, they seek employment from private

A college student working as a waiter takes a family's order. Many students work for private employers, such as restaurants, to help pay for college.

employers. For many part-time positions, college students are often highly sought after by private employers. Students have relatively flexible schedules. They are also not seeking a full-time position and will accept lower wages and no benefits, such as health care or a retirement plan. Common part-time jobs you may want to consider are restaurant server or kitchen worker, retail sales clerk, tutor, baby sitter, and seasonal worker.

Private employment has a financial downside, when compared to a federal work-study job. The money you earn from a private employer will be considered as income on your FAFSA application the following year, which may affect the amount of financial aid you receive. For many students, however, income earned through employment results in lowering the amount of student loans.

College Board A nonprofit educational organization with more than six thousand member colleges and educational organizations; it administers the SAT and provides college admissions and financial aid information to students.

cosigner A person who jointly signs a promissory note for a loan, assuming responsibility for repaying the loan if the primary borrower fails to repay it.

cost of attendance The total amount of college expenses, including tuition, fees, room and board, books, and living expenses.

defer To postpone payment of a loan for a period of time; for many student loans, repayment is postponed until the student graduates from college.

educational loan Money a student borrows from the government, a financial institution, or other source to pay for college; the money must be paid back, usually with interest.

expected family contribution The amount of money a family is expected to contribute to a student's college costs each year; calculated using information supplied on the FAFSA.

financial aid Money given or lent to a student to help pay for college; includes scholarships and grants, loans, and work-study programs.

financial aid officer A college employee who helps students apply for and receive financial aid and answers questions about the financial aid process.

financial need The difference between a student's expected family contribution and the cost of attendance.

529 saving plan Tax-free, state-sponsored investment plan that helps families pay for college.

Free Application for Federal Student Aid (FAFSA) A form required for all students seeking federal student grants, loans, and work-study aid; many college financial aid offices also require it for college-based financial aid.

grant A type of financial aid, usually based on financial need, that a student does not have to repay.

interest The fee that a borrower pays for the use of borrowed money.

loan Funds transferred from a lender to a borrower with an agreement that the borrower pay back the amount borrowed, plus interest, over a specific period of time.

loan servicer A company that handles the billing and customer service for the repayment of a loan.

promissory note A legal contract between a lender and a borrower that contains the terms and condition of a loan.

scholarship A type of financial aid, usually based on merit, that a student does not have to repay.

Student Aid Report (SAR) The U.S. Department of Education report sent to students and colleges that shows a student's expected family contribution; calculated from information provided by the student on the FAFSA application.

work-study program A financial aid program that enables students to work at a part-time job, often on campus, to earn money to pay for college.

Army Reserve Officers' Training Corps (Army ROTC)
1400 Defense Pentagon
Washington, DC 20301-1400
(888) 550-2769
Website: http://www.goarmy.com/rotc.html
Army ROTC provides information about Reserve
    Officers' Training Corps scholarships available through
    the U.S. Army.

Canada Education Savings Program
140 Promenade du Portage, Phase IV
Mailstop: Bag 4
Gatineau, QC K1A 0J9
Canada
(800) 622-6232
Website: http://www.canlearn.ca
This division of Canada's Department of Employment and
    Social Development Canada provides information on
    college saving programs available in Canada and guid-
    ance on other educational planning topics.

College Board
45 Columbus Avenue
New York, NY 10023-6992
(212) 713-8000
Website: www.collegeboard.org
This nonprofit testing and education company administers the
    CSS/Profile and provides information on financial aid.

Mapping Your Future
P.O. Box 5176
Round Rock, TX 78683-5176
(940) 497-0741
Website: http://www.mappingyourfuture.org
This nonprofit organization provides career, college, and fi-
nancial aid information and services for students, fami-
lies, and schools.

National Association of Student Financial Aid Administrators
1101 Connecticut Avenue NW, Suite 1100
Washington, DC 20036-4303
(202) 785-0453
Website: http://www.nasfaa.org
This nonprofit organization of college financial assistance
professionals provides advocates for increased access to
student financial aid and provides information about
financial aid to students and parents.

National Merit Scholarship Corporation
1560 Sherman Avenue
Suite 200
Evanston, IL 60201-4897
(847) 866-5100
Website: http://www.nationalmerit.org
This nonprofit organization sponsors two major scholarship
programs: the National Merit Scholarship Program
and the National Achievement Scholarship Program.

National Student Loans Service Centre
P.O. Box 4030
Mississauga, ON L5A 4M4
Canada
(888) 815-4514
Website: http://www.hrsdc.gc.ca/eng/jobs/student/loans_grants
This division of Canada's Department of Employment and Social
Development administers student loans and grants and
provides information on various types of financial aid avail-
able in Canada.

Sallie Mae
P.O. Box 9500
Wilkes-Barre, PA 18773-9500
(888) 272-5543
Website: https://www.salliemae.com
This company provides private educational loans and services and
federal, state, and private student loans. Its website provides
general information on financial aid.

Telluride Association
217 West Avenue
Ithaca, NY 14850
(607) 273-5011
Website: http://www.tellurideassociation.org
This nonprofit organization helps students develop skills in
leadership and public service and sponsors several scholarship programs.

U.S. Department of Education
P.O. Box 84
Washington, DC 20044-0084
(800) 433-3243
Website: http://studentaid.ed.gov
This federal government agency provides funds for financial aid,
    administers the Free Application for Federal Student Aid,
    and provides general information about financial aid.

U.S Department of Labor
200 Constitution Avenue NW
Washington, DC 20210
(866) 487-2365
Website: http://www.dol.gov
This federal agency maintains an online scholarship search
    tool and provides information on jobs and careers.

WEBSITES

Due to the changing nature of Internet links, Rosen Publishing
has developed an online list of websites related to the subject of
this book. This site is updated regularly. Please use this link to
access the list:

http://www.rosenlinks.com/FSLS/Pay

Axe, David. *Army 101: Inside ROTC in a Time of War.* Columbia, SC: University of South Carolina Press, 2007.

Bissonnette, Zac. *Debt-Free U: How I Paid for an Outstanding College Education Without Loans, Scholarships, or Mooching Off My Parents.* New York, NY: Penguin, 2011.

Brown, Stewart. *The Student Athlete's Guide to Getting Recruited: How to Win Scholarships, Attract Colleges and Excel as an Athlete.* Belmont, CA: SuperCollege, 2011.

Butler, Tamsen. *The Complete Guide to Personal Finance: For Teenagers and College Students.* Ocala, FL: Atlantic, 2011.

Chany, Kalman. *Paying for College Without Going Broke.* New York, NY: Princeton Review, 2012.

Clark, Ken. *The Complete Idiot's Guide to Paying for College.* New York, NY: Alpha, 2010.

College Board. *College Handbook 2014.* New York, NY: College Board, 2013.

College Board. *Getting Financial Aid 2014.* New York, NY: College Board, 2013.

College Board. *Scholarship Handbook 2014.* New York, NY: College Board, 2013.

Collinge, Alan Michael. *The Student Loan Scam: The Most Oppressive Debt in U.S. History and How We Can Fight Back.* Boston, MA: Beacon Press, 2009.

Ellis, Kristina. *Confessions of a Scholarship Winner: The Secrets That Helped Me Win $500,000 in Free Money for College.* Brentwood, TN: Worthy, 2013.

Hahn, Kathy Lynn. *The Complete Guide to Writing Effective College Applications and Essays for Admission and Scholarships.* Ocala, FL: Atlantic, 2009.

Hurley, Joseph F. *The Best Way to Save for College: A Complete Guide to 529 Plans 2013–14.* Pittsford, NY: Saving for College, 2013.

McCormick, Lisa. *Financial Aid Smarts: Getting Money for School.* New York, NY: Rosen, 2013.

Peterson's. *Paying for College: Answers to All Your Questions About Financial Aid, Tuition Payment Plans, and Everything Else You Need to Know.* Lawrenceville, NJ: Peterson's, 2008.

Peterson's. *Scholarships, Grants, & Prizes.* Lawrenceville, NJ: Peterson's, 2013.

Ragins, Marianne. *Winning Scholarships for College.* New York, NY: Holt, 2013.

Stone, Elliott H. *Student Loan Secrets "They" Don't Want You to Know About.* Santa Ana, CA: California Consumer Law Center, 2013.

Tanabe, Gen and Kelly Tanabe. *The Ultimate Scholarship Book 2014.* Belmont, CA: SuperCollege, 2013.

Carnevale, Anthony P., Jeff Strohl, and Michelle Melton. "What's It Worth?: The Economic Value of College Majors." 2011. Retrieved January 13, 2014 (http://www9.georgetown.edu/grad/gppi/hpi/cew/pdfs/whatsitworth-complete.pdf).

Carrns, Anne. "New Student Loan Rules Add Protections for Borrowers." 2013. Retrieved January 20, 2014 (http://www.nytimes.com/2013/11/06/your-money/new-student-loan-rules-add-protections-for-borrowers.html).

Cohen, Steven, Anne Dwane, Paulo de Oliveira, and Michael Muska. *Getting In! College Admissions and Financial Aid in the Digital Age.* Hoboken, NJ: Wiley, 2011.

Cohen, Steve. "Paying for College (When You Haven't Saved Enough)." 2010. Retrieved January 10, 2014 (http://www.forbes.com/sites/stevecohen/2010/10/09/paying-for-college-when-you-havent-saved-enough).

College Board. "The Basics on Grants and Scholarships." Retrieved January 16, 2014 (https://bigfuture.collegeboard.org/pay-for-college/grants-and-scholarships/the-basics-on-grants-and-scholarships).

College Board. "Types of College Loans." Retrieved January 20, 2014 (https://bigfuture.collegeboard.org/pay-for-college/loans/types-of-college-loans).

Herzog, Karen. "Working Your Way Through College Doesn't Add Up for Today's Students." 2013. Retrieved January 19, 2014 (http://www.jsonline.com/news/education/working-your-way-through-college-doesnt-add-up-for-todays-students-b9922857z1-209807931.html).

Illinois Student Assistance Commission. "Free Application
for Federal Student Aid (FAFSA)." 2014. Retrieved
January 13, 2014 (http://www.isac.org/students/during
-college/applying-for-financial-aid/free-application-for
-federal-student-aid-fafsa.html).

Kamenetz, Anya. "How to Get Out of Default on a Student
Loan." 2013. Retrieved January 20, 2014 (http://www
.chicagotribune.com/business/sns-201309101900--tms
--savingsgctnzy-a20130910-20130910,0,2500170.story).

Lucier, Kelci Lynn. "Consider Pros and Cons of Working in
College." 2012. Retrieved January 19, 2014 (http://www
.usnews.com/education/best-colleges/articles/2012/09/13/
consider-pros-and-cons-of-working-in-college).

Onick, Troy. "2013 Guide to FAFSA, CSS Profile, Expected
Family Contribution (EFC) and College Aid." 2013.
Retrieved January 20, 2014 (http://www.forbes.com/
sites/troyonink/2013/01/02/2013-simplified-guide-to
-expected-family-contribution-efc-and-college-aid).

Perna, Laura W. "Understanding the Working College Student."
2010. Retrieved January 19, 2014 (http://www.aaup.org/
article/understanding-working-college-student#
.Us18xvuAffg).

Sallie Mae. "How America Pays for College 2013." 2013.
Retrieved January 15, 2013 (https://www.salliemae
.com/assets/Core/how-America-pays/
howamericapays2013.pdf).

Scholarship America. "5 Reasons Why Scholarships Are
Essential." 2011. Retrieved January 14, 2013 (http://www

.usnews.com/education/blogs/the-scholarship-coach/ 2011/07/07/5-reasons-why-scholarships-are-essential).

Scholarship America. "3 Hot Scholarship Trends to Watch for in 2014." 2013. Retrieved January 16, 2014 (http:// www.usnews.com/education/blogs/the-scholarship -coach/2013/11/07/3-hot-scholarship-trends-to -watch-for-in-2014).

Stack, Carol, and Ruth Vedvik. *The Financial Aid Handbook*. Pompton Plains, NJ: Career Press, 2011.

Tanabe, Gen, and Kelly Tanabe. *How to Pay for College*. Belmont, CA: SuperCollege, 2011.

U.S. Army. "ROTC: Ways to Attend." Retrieved January 20, 2014 (http://www.goarmy.com/rotc/ways-to-attend.html).

U.S. Department of Education. "Federal Pell Grants." Retrieved January 14, 2013 (http://studentaid.ed.gov/types/grants -scholarships/pell).

U.S. Department of Education. "Finding and Applying for Scholarships." Retrieved January 14, 2014 (http:// studentaid.ed.gov/types/grants-scholarships/finding -scholarships).

INDEX

ABOUT THE AUTHOR

G. S. Prentzas has written more than thirty books for young readers, including *How Interest Rates, Credit Ratings, and Lending Affect You* and *Essential Careers as a Paralegal and Legal Assistant* for Rosen Publishing. He graduated from the University of North Carolina and the University of North Carolina School of Law.

PHOTO CREDITS

Cover, p. 3 © iStockphoto.com/amanalang (beverage server), © iStockphoto .com/RyanJLane (background); pp. 6–7 The Christian Science Monitor/ Getty Images; p. 10 James Woodson/Photodisc/Thinkstock; p. 12 altrendo images/Stockbyte/Getty Images; pp. 13, 41 © AP Images; p. 17 Konstantin Yoishin/Shutterstock.com; p. 19 Larry St. Pierre/Shutterstock.com; p. 21 PRNewsFoto/Comcast/AP Images; p. 23 Blend Images KidStock/Brand X Pictures/Getty Images; p. 24 Darren Abate/AP Images for US Army; p. 29 SimplyCreativePhotography/E+/Getty Images; p. 31 Monkey Business Images/Shutterstock.com; p. 34 Centre Daily Times/McClatchy-Tribune/ Getty Images; p. 35 Scott Leigh/E+/Getty Images; p. 39 Ralf Hirschberger/ picture-alliance/dpa/AP Images; p. 46 sturti/E+/Getty Images; p. 49 michaeljung/Shutterstock.com; p. 51 Blend Images/Ariel Skelley/Vetta/ Getty Images; p. 52 Jupiterimages/Stockbyte/Thinkstock; p. 55 Mark Bowden/E+/Getty Images; p. 61 kali9/E+/Getty Images; p. 62 Wavebreakmedia Ltd/Thinkstock; p. 65 Yellow Dog Productions/The Image Bank/Getty Images; interior page design elements © iStockphoto.com/ yystom (arrows), © iStockphoto.com/JLGutierrez (financial terms), © iStockphoto.com/ahlobystov (numbers).

Designer: Nelson Sá; Editor: Shalini Saxena;
Photo Researcher: Karen Huang